Other Helen Exley Giftbooks:

Ms Murphy's Law   A Bouquet of Wedding Jokes
To my Husband with Love   The Little Book of Stress
The Wicked Little Book of Quotes   True Love...

Published simultaneously in 1998 by Exley Publications Ltd in Great Britain,
and Exley Publications LLC in the USA.

12 11 10 9 8 7 6 5 4 3 2 1

Border illustrations by Juliette Clarke.
Edited and pictures selected by Helen Exley.
© Helen Exley 1998
The moral right of the author has been asserted.

ISBN: 1-86187-069-8

Exley Publications Ltd, 16 Chalk Hill, Watford, Herts WD1 4BN, UK.
Exley Publications LLC, 232 Madison Avenue, Suite 1206, NY 10016, USA.

MEN!
by women

A HELEN EXLEY GIFTBOOK

EXLEY
NEW YORK · WATFORD, UK

How can you tell when a man has insomnia?
He keeps waking up every few days.

How many men does it take to change a roll of toilet
paper? We don't know, it's never happened.

What do you call a man who complains all day,
watches sport all night and sleeps away his weekends?
Normal.

NAN TUCKET

What's a man's idea of helping with housework? Lifting his legs so you can vacuum.

NAN TUCKET

It's not the men in my life that count,
it's the life in my men.

MAE WEST (1893-1980)

I'm looking for a perfume to overpower men
— I'm sick of karate.

PHYLLIS DILLER

A girl can wait for the right man
to come along, but in the meantime
that still doesn't mean she can't have fun
with all the wrong ones.

CHER

You can let off steam to him and rant and rage, and he'll look up from his newspaper and say "Did you say something dear?"

ANN WEBB

If love means never having to say you're sorry, then marriage means always having to say everything twice.

ESTELLE GETTY

What's the thinnest book in the world?
What Men Know About Women.

NAN TUCKET

Women speak because they wish to speak, whereas
a man speaks only when driven to speech by
something outside himself — like, for instance, he
can't find any clean socks.

JEAN KERR, b.1923

POOR GUYS!

Any person can tell, when they look around at men in general, that God never intended women to be very particular.

ANONYMOUS SUFFRAGIST

I know God is not a woman – no woman would have created men with so many imperfections.

JILL M. CONSIDEINE

Women want mediocre men, and men are working to be as mediocre as possible.

MARGARET MEAD (1901-1978)

I love men!
I love their money!

I am a marvelous housekeeper.

Every time I leave a man I keep his house.

ZSA ZSA GABOR, b.1919

Why is it no one ever sent me yet

One perfect limousine, do you suppose?

Ah no, it's always just my luck to

get one perfect rose.

DOROTHY PARKER (1893-1967)

I never hated a man enough to give him his diamonds back.

ZSA ZSA GABOR, b.1919

Where's the man could ease the heart
Like a satin gown?

DOROTHY PARKER (1893-1967)

I like men who are
prematurely wealthy.

JOAN RIVERS, b.1933

WE LOVE THEM.
WE JUST DO.

*I require only three things
in a man.
He must be handsome, ruthless,
and stupid.*

DOROTHY PARKER (1893-1967)

I like men to behave like men –
strong and childish.

FRANCOISE SAGAN, b.1935

Men are those creatures with two legs
and eight hands.

JAYNE MANSFIELD (1932-1967)

The only place men want depth
in a woman
is in her décolletage.

ZSA ZSA GABOR, b.1919

A gentleman is a patient wolf.

HENRIETTE TIARKS

Give a man a free hand and he'll run it
all over you.

MAE WEST (1893-1980)

What's the definition of a bad date?
You pay for the dinner and he still
runs out of gas.

NAN TUCKET

Personally, I think if a woman hasn't met the right man by the time she's 24, she may be lucky.

JEAN KERR, b.1923

As soon as a man says "I do," he don't.

CYNTHIA NELMS

Bigamy is having one husband too many. Monogamy is the same.

NAN TUCKET

Why are men better than dogs?
Men only have two feet that track in mud.

JENNIFER BERMAN

What's the difference between men and pigs?
One likes to eat, sleep, burp, and roll in the mud;
the other is considered intelligent,
and has a curly tail and a snout.

NAN TUCKET

*Men should be sent to an island
where they can walk around in ripped underwear
and drink milk out of cartons until they drop.*

SUSAN DEY

*Gardening men wash their hands when they
come in. In the process of which they transfer
the mud to the basin, the soap, the facecloth and
the towel. And leave it there as evidence
of the hard morning's work.*

PAM BROWN, b.1928

A MODERN CENTAUR: HALF A MAN AND HALF A SPORTSCAR.

EDITH GROBLEBEN

[Men] have such wonderful minds.
So much is stored inside —
all those sports scores and so on.

JANE SEYMOUR

Vive la

I'm not denyin' that women are foolish;
God Almighty made 'em to match the men.

GEORGE ELIOT (MARY ANN EVANS)
(1819-1880)

A man has to be Joe McCarthy to be called
ruthless. All a woman has to do
is put you on hold.

MARLO THOMAS, b.1943

différence!

A woman has to consider whether her dress
is too short, her trousers too tight, her V-neck
too low, whether her legs are shaved, her lipstick
is on right, whether her hair looks best
up or down.
A man makes sure his zipper is closed
and gets on stage.

RACHEL BERGER

No man has ever had an ordinary cold.

PAM BROWN, b.1928

He was like a cock who thought the sun had risen to hear him crow.

GEORGE ELIOT (MARY ANN EVANS)
(1819-1880)

WE HAD A LOT IN COMMON,
I LOVED HIM AND HE LOVED HIM.

SHELLEY WINTERS

Two angels decide how humans
should reproduce: "If the females have
the babies, the men will feel really inferior
– we'll give them enormous egos
to make up for it."

CATHY AND MO

Only a man could instigate the idea
that a woman's happiness lies
in serving and pleasing a man.

MARGARET FULLER (1810-1850)

Oh dear me – it's too late to do anything
but accept you and love you – but when
you were quite a little boy somebody
ought to have said "hush" just once!

BEATRICE CAMPBELL (1865-1940)
TO GEORGE BERNARD SHAW

You can't change a man, no-ways. By the time his mummy turns him loose and he takes up with some innocent woman and marries her, he's what he is.

MARJORIE KINNAN RAWLINGS

The only time a woman succeeds in changing a man is when he's a baby.

NATALIE WOOD (1938-1982)

"THE HUSBAND"

THE TROUBLE
WITH SOME WOMEN
IS THAT THEY GET ALL EXCITED
ABOUT NOTHING —
AND THEN MARRY HIM.

CHER

Before marriage
a man will lay awake all night
thinking about something
you said; after marriage,
he'll fall asleep before you finish
saying it.

HELEN ROWLAND (1875-1950)

A man in love
is incomplete until
he has married.
Then he is finished.

ZSA ZSA GABOR, b.1919

Most women
set out to try to change a man,
and when they have changed him
they do not like him.

MARLENE DIETRICH (1904-1992)

My ancestors
wandered lost in the wilderness
for forty years
because even in biblical times,
men would not stop to ask
for directions.

ELAYNE BOOSLER

Teddies are better

[Teddy bears] never interrupt; never tell you to snap out of it; never come up with some ditzy, smart-alec solution to all your problems. They are sympathetic and silent and never, never disappear for the day to play golf.

ABIGAIL HARMAN

I never married because I have three
pets at home that answer the same
purpose as a husband. I have a dog
that growls every morning, a parrot
that swears all afternoon, and a cat
that comes home late at night.

MARIE CORELLI (1855-1924)

WHY DOGS ARE BETTER THAN MEN

Dogs admit it when they're lost.

Dogs are nice to your relatives.

Dogs aren't threatened if you earn more than they do.

Dogs do not care whether you shave your legs.

Dogs don't step on the imaginary brake.

Dogs don't mind if you do all the driving.

Middle-aged dogs don't feel the need to abandon you

for a younger dog.

Dogs don't correct your stories.

Dogs do not read at the table.

The worst social disease you can get from dogs is fleas.

Dogs don't feel threatened by your intelligence.

JENNIFER BERMAN

A good man doesn't just happen.

They have to be created by women.

A guy is a lump, like a donut. So first you gotta

get rid of all the stuff his mom did to him. And

then you gotta get rid of all that macho crap

they pick up from beer commercials.

And then there's my favorite, the male ego.

ROSEANNE BARR

SEXY THINGS!

I only like two kinds
of men: domestic
and imported.

MAE WEST (1893-1980)

*I'd like to get married because
I like the idea of a man being
required by law to sleep with me
every night.*

CARRIE SNOW

*I feel like a million —
but one at a time.*

MAE WEST (1893-1980)

*Italians are obsessed
by two things.
The other one is spaghetti.*

CATHERINE DENEUVE, b.1943

*Every man wants a woman to appeal
to his better side and his nobler instincts
— and another woman to help him
forget them.*

HELEN ROWLAND (1875-1950)

*It isn't tying himself to one woman that
a man dreads when he thinks
of marrying; it's separating himself
from all the others.*

HELEN ROWLAND (1875-1950)

*I wouldn't trust my husband
with a young woman for five minutes,
and he's been dead for twenty five years.*

BRENDAN BEHAN'S MOTHER

A husband is the bloke
that sticks with you through the troubles
you wouldn't have had if you hadn't married
him in the first place.

CAROLINE AMMERLAAN

A woman who strives to be like a man
lacks ambition.

AUTHOR UNKNOWN

I refuse to consign the whole male sex
to the nursery. I insist on believing that
some men are my equals.

BRIGID BROPHY

JUST FLATTER HIM!

*Women have served all these centuries
as looking-glasses possessing the magic
and delicious power of reflecting the figure
of a man twice its natural size.*

VIRGINIA WOOLF (1882-1941)

The average man is more interested in a woman who is interested in him than he is in a woman – any woman – with beautiful legs.

MARLENE DIETRICH (1904-1992)

... I think if it would help condom efficiency, we should package them in different sizes, and maybe label them like olives: jumbo, colossal, and super-colossal, so that men don't have to go in and ask for the small.

BARBARA SEAMAN, b.1935

A man loves a woman so much, he asks her to marry — to change her name, quit her job, have and raise the babies, be home when he gets there, move where his job is. You can hardly imagine what he might ask if he didn't love her.

GABRIELLE BURTON

Why do men watch football?
Because it'd be boring to talk about sex
all the time.

NAN TUCKET

Some men believe that every woman's
secret desire is to have the fine points
of football demonstrated with
the silverware.

JANE CAMPBELL

If a man watches three football matches in a row, he should be declared legally dead.

ERMA BOMBECK, b.1927

If you never want to see a man again, say, "I love you. I want to marry you. I want to have children" — they leave skid marks.

RITA RUDNER

The Kitchen Wars

My husband says he wants to spend his vacation someplace he's never been before. I said, "How about the kitchen?"

NAN TUCKET

A man is the one who has one surefire,
extra-special, hey-presto recipe which
entails a whole lot of dirty dishes.

PAM BROWN, b.1928

... no matter how satisfactory any life is
in its broad sweep, there will always be
moments of anguish, always causes for
panic, concern, rage and bewilderment.
Many of them will be in a kitchen
with a man in it.

BARBARA TONER

IDIOTS!

*More husbands would leave home
if they knew how to pack.*

CAROLINE AMMERLAAN

God gave women
intuition and femininity.
Used properly
the combination easily
jumbles the brain of any
man I've ever met.

FARRAH FAWCETT

Acknowledgements: The Publishers are grateful for permission to reproduce copyright material. Whilst every reasonable effort has been made to trace copyright holders, the publishers would be pleased to hear from any not here acknowledged. CAROLINE AMMERLAAN: From *Women on Men*, ed. Caroline Ammerlaan. Published by Axiom Publishers, South Australia. JENNIFER BERMAN: From *Why Dogs Are Better Than Men*, published by Simon and Schuster (Pocket Books).©1993 Jennifer Berman. ABIGAIL HARMAN: From *Shooting Teddy Bears is No Picnic* by A. Harman. ©1993 Abigail Harman. BARBARA TONER: From *A Mother's Guide to Life*, published by Hodder, 1997. ©1997 Barbara Toner. NAN TUCKET: From *All Men Are Bastards Joke Book*, published originally by Warner Books, Inc. Published by Pan Macmillan in the UK. ©1992 Nan Tucket. BETTY JANE WYLIE: From *Men! Quotations About Men, By Women*, ed. Betty Jane Wylie. Published by Key Porter Books Ltd. ©1993 Betty Jane Wylie.